BLENDED
WORSHIP 2

12 Praise and Worship Songs with 12 Praise and Worship Hymns Arranged in 12 Medleys

Arranged and Orchestrated by
Camp Kirkland and Richard Kingsmore

lillenas
PUBLISHING COMPANY

lillenas.com

Contents in Sequence

Alphabetical Index

Forever

with

O God, Our Help in Ages Past

Words and Music by
CHRIS TOMLIN
Arr. by Camp Kirkland

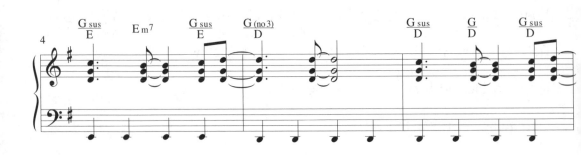

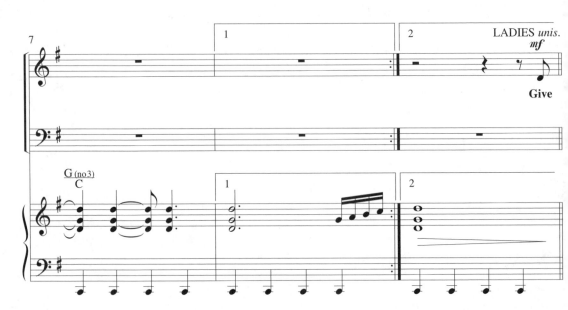

10

49 *"O God, Our Help in Ages Past"

CD: 5

(to pg. 11, meas. 65)

Indescribable

with

Praise Him! Praise Him!

LAURA STORY and
JESSE REEVES

LAURA STORY
Arr. by Richard Kingsmore

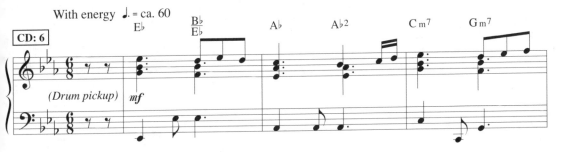

From the high-est of heights to the depths of the

sea

Cre - a - tion's re -

47

LADIES *unis.*

Who i - mag-ined the sun and gives source to its light,

50

CD: 9

Yet con-ceals it to bring us the cool-ness of

53

D.S. al Coda CODA
CHOIR *unis.* (to pg. 15, meas. 21)
CD: 10

night? None can fath - om: God!

*"Praise Him! Praise Him!"

83

Tell of His ex - cel - lent great - ness. Praise Him!

Fm | A♭/B♭ | E♭ | A♭2/E♭ | E♭ | E♭/D♭

86

CD: 12

Praise Him! ev - er in joy - ful song!

A♭/C | A♭m6/C♭ | E♭/B♭ B♭ E♭/B♭ E♭/B♭ | B♭7 C sus | C

89

f

In - de - scrib - a - ble! Un - con - tain - a - ble!

f

F | C | C sus

Awe - struck, we fall to our knees as we hum - bly pro - claim:

You are a - maz - ing God!

You are a - maz - ing God!

We Fall Down

with
O Come, Let Us Adore Him

Words and Music by
CHRIS TOMLIN
Arr. by Richard Kingsmore

1st time: LADIES *unis.*
2nd time: CHOIR *unis.*

"O Come, Let Us Adore Him"

O come, let us a - dore Him, O
(We'll) praise His name for - ev - er, We'll

come, let us a - dore Him, O come, let us a -
praise His name for - ev - er, We'll praise His name for -

30

(to pg. 29, meas. 25)
CHOIR unis.

dore Him,____ Christ_____ the Lord.
ev - er,____ Christ_____ the We'll

mf

B♭ B♭/A♭ E♭2/G F m7 E♭/B♭ B♭sus B♭ A♭/B♭ E♭ B♭/E♭ A♭/E♭

(to pg. 29, meas. 25)

f

Lord. We'll give Him all the glo - ry, We'll

f

cresc.

B A/B E B/E F♯m⁷₄ F♯m E/G♯ A 2 A M7/B

f

give Him all the glo - ry, We'll give Him all the

E B/D♯ C♯m7 A E/G♯ E/A B E F♯m7 E/G♯ F♯m/A F♯7/A♯

48

CD: 19

Christ_____ the Lord.

We fall__ down,__ we

lay our__ crowns__ at the feet_____ of Je -

Beautiful One

with
O Worship the King

Words and Music by
TIM HUGHES
Arr. by Camp Kirkland

40

*"O Worship the King"

soul must sing. Beau-ti-ful

One my soul must sing.

Sing to the King

with
Joyful, Joyful, We Adore Thee

Words and Music by
BILL JAMES FOOTE and
CHARLES SILVESTER HORNE
Arr. by Richard Kingsmore

CD: 31 1st time

CD: 33 2nd time

a song,___ a song de - clar - ing that we___

be - long___ to Je - sus,___ He is all___ we

need. Lift up a heart___

*"Joyful, Joyful, We Adore Thee"

Joy - ful, joy - ful, we a - dore Thee,

God of glo - ry, Lord of love; Hearts un - fold like

flow'rs be - fore Thee, Open - ing to the sun a - bove.

Melt the clouds of sin and__ sad - ness; Drive the__ dark of

doubt a - way. Giv - er of im - mor - tal glad - ness,

CD: 35

CD: 36

In the tri-umph song of life!

Come, let us sing a song, a

song de-clar-ing that we be-long to Je-sus,

Enough

with
I Need Thee Every Hour

Words and Music by
CHRIS TOMLIN
and LOUIE GIGLIO
Arr. by Richard Kingsmore

1. You are my sup-ply, my breath of life;
2. You're my sac-ri-fice of great-est price;

is more than e-nough___ for ___ all of me,___

for___ ev - 'ry thirst___ and ___ ev - 'ry need.___

You___ sat - is - fy___ me ___ with Your love,___

and all I have in You is more than e - nough.

CD: 40

(to pg. 58, meas. 5)

CD: 42

(to pg. 58, meas. 5)

62

The Heart of Worship

with

My Jesus, I Love Thee

Words and Music by
MATT REDMAN
Arr. by Camp Kirkland

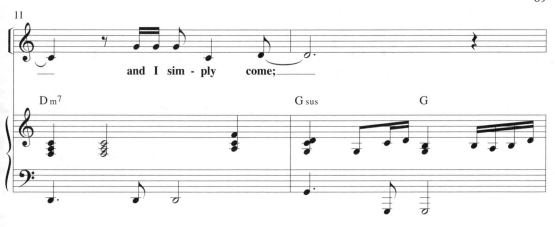

and I sim - ply come;

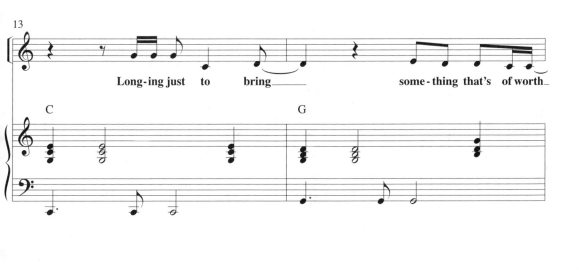

Long-ing just to bring_____ some - thing that's of worth__

that will bless Your heart._____

Blessed Be Your Name

with
It Is Well with My Soul

Words and Music by
MATT REDMAN
and BETH REDMAN
Arr. by Camp Kirkland

L.H. can be played as eighth notes

82

1st time: MEN *parts*
2nd time: ALL

You give and take a - way, You give and take a - way,___ My heart will choose to say, Lord, bless - ed be Your name.___ You

Once Again

with
I Will Praise Him

Words and Music by
MATT REDMAN
Arr. by Camp Kirkland

CD: 64

Warmly ♩ = ca. 70

1st time: CHOIR unis.
2nd time: LADIES unis.

1. Je - sus Christ,__ I think up - on Your sac - ri - fice,
2. Now You are__ ex - alt - ed to the high - est place,

94

CD: 70

Once a-gain I thank You, once a-gain I pour out my life.

Thank You for the cross. Thank You for the cross.

Holy Is the Lord

with

Holy, Holy, Holy! Lord God Almighty!

Words and Music by
CHRIS TOMLIN
and LOUIE GIGLIO
Arr. by Camp Kirkland

ALL *both times*

We bow down___ and wor-

- ship Him now;___ How great,___ how awe - some is He!

___ And to-geth - er we___ sing,___

*"Holy, Holy, Holy! Lord God Almighty!"

Ho - ly, ho - ly, ho - ly! Lord God Al - might - y!

(to pg. 97, meas. 5)

CD: 78

You Are My King

with
Amazing Grace

Words and Music by
BILLY JAMES FOOTE
Arr. by Richard Kingsmore

1st time: SOLO *(or Choir unis.)*
2nd time: CHOIR *unis.*

I'm for-giv - en be-cause You were_ for-sak - en._ I'm ac-cept - ed,_

112

114

gun.

A-maz-ing love, how____ can it be____

That You, my King__ would die__ for me?____

A - maz - ing love,___ I_____ know it's true.

F   B♭2

CD: 88 *1st time*

1   (to pg. 116, meas. 63)

It's my joy___ to hon - or You.___

F   1   (to pg. 116, meas. 63)
C sus   C

2

In all___ I do_____ I hon - or You.__

2
C sus   C   B♭2   C⁷sus   C⁷

He Is Exalted

with
Immortal, Invisible, God Only Wise

Words and Music by
TWILA PARIS
Arr. by Richard Kingsmore